P9-AQX-968

Page to be Filled

Russia in the Shadows

STREET SCENERY IN PETERSBURG: SITE OF A DEMOLISHED
WOODEN HOUSE.

Frontispiece.

Russia in the Shadows

By
H. G. Wells

HODDER AND STOUGHTON
LIMITED   LONDON

Contents

I. Petersburg in Collapse

I. Petersburg in Collapse

IN January 1914 I visited Petersburg and Moscow for a couple of weeks; in September 1920 I was asked to repeat this visit by Mr. Kamenev, of the Russian Trade Delegation in London. I snatched at this suggestion, and went to Russia at the end of September with my son, who speaks a little Russian. We spent a fortnight and a day in Russia, passing most of our time in Petersburg, where we went about freely by ourselves, and were shown nearly everything we asked to see. We visited Moscow, and I had a long conversation with Mr. Lenin, which I shall relate. In Petersburg I did not stay at the Hotel International, to which foreign visitors are usually sent, but with my old friend, Maxim Gorky. The guide and interpreter assigned to assist us was a lady I had met in Russia in 1914, the niece of a former Russian Ambassador to London. She was educated at Newnham, she has been imprisoned five times by the Bolshevist Government, she is not allowed to leave Petersburg because of an attempt to cross the frontier to her children in Esthonia, and she was, therefore, the last person likely to lend herself to any attempt to hoodwink me. I mention this because on every hand at home and in Russia I had been told that the most elaborate camouflage of realities would go on, and that I should be kept in blinkers throughout my visit.

As a matter of fact, the harsh and terrible realities of the situation in Russia cannot be camouflaged. In the case of special delegations, perhaps, a certain distracting tumult of receptions, bands, and speeches may be possible, and may be attempted. But it is hardly possible to dress up two large cities for the benefit of two stray visitors, wandering observantly often in different directions. Naturally, when one demands to see a school or a prison one is not shown the worst. Any country would in the circumstances show the best it had, and Soviet Russia is no exception. One can allow for that.

Our dominant impression of things Russian is an impression of a vast irreparable breakdown. The great monarchy that was here in 1914, the administrative, social, financial, and commercial systems connected with it have, under the strains of six years of incessant war, fallen down and smashed utterly. Never in all history has there been so great a *débâcle* before. The fact of the Revolution is, to our minds, altogether dwarfed by the fact of this downfall. By its own inherent rottenness and by the thrusts and strains of aggressive imperialism the Russian part of the old civilised world that existed before 1914 fell, and is now gone. The peasant, who was the base of the old pyramid, remains upon the land, living very much as he has always lived. Everything else is broken down, or is breaking down. Amid this vast disorganisation an emer-

gency Government, supported by a disciplined party of perhaps 150,000 adherents
—the Communist Party—has taken control. It has—at the price of much shooting
—suppressed brigandage, established a sort
of order and security in the exhausted
towns, and set up a crude rationing
system.

It is, I would say at once, the only
possible Government in Russia at the
present time. It is the only idea, it
supplies the only solidarity, left in Russia.
But it is a secondary fact. The dominant
fact for the Western reader, the threatening
and disconcerting fact, is that a social and
economic system very like our own and
intimately connected with our own has
crashed.

Nowhere in all Russia is the fact of that
crash so completely evident as it is in
Petersburg. Petersburg was the artificial
creation of Peter the Great ; his bronze
statue in the little garden near the Admiralty still prances amid the ebbing life of
the city. Its palaces are still and empty,

or strangely refurnished with the type-writers and tables and plank partitions of a new Administration which is engaged chiefly in a strenuous struggle against famine and the foreign invader. Its streets were streets of busy shops. In 1914 I loafed agreeably in the Petersburg streets—buying little articles and watching the abundant traffic. All these shops have ceased. There are perhaps half a dozen shops still open in Petersburg. There is a Government crockery shop where I bought a plate or so as a souvenir, for seven or eight hundred roubles each, and there are a few flower shops. It is a wonderful fact, I think, that in this city, in which most of the shrinking population is already nearly starving, and hardly any one possesses a second suit of clothes or more than a single change of worn and patched linen, flowers can be and are still bought and sold. For five thousand roubles, which is about six and eightpence at the current rate of exchange, one can get a very pleasing bunch of big chrysanthemums.

I do not know if the words " all the shops have ceased " convey any picture to the Western reader of what a street looks like in Russia. It is not like Bond Street or Piccadilly on a Sunday, with the blinds neatly drawn down in a decorous sleep, and ready to wake up and begin again on Monday. The shops have an utterly wretched and abandoned look ; paint is peeling off, windows are cracked, some are broken and boarded up, some still display a few fly-blown relics of stock in the window, some have their windows covered with notices ; the windows are growing dim, the fixtures have gathered two years' dust. They are dead shops. They will never open again.

All the great bazaar-like markets are closed, too, in Petersburg now, in the desperate struggle to keep a public control of necessities and prevent the profiteer driving up the last vestiges of food to incredible prices. And this cessation of shops makes walking about the streets seem a silly sort of thing to do. Nobody

" walks about " any more. One realises
that a modern city is really nothing but
long alleys of shops and restaurants and
the like. Shut them up, and the meaning
of a street has disappeared. People hurry
past—a thin traffic compared with my
memories of 1914. The electric street
cars are still running and busy—until six
o'clock. They are the only means of
locomotion for ordinary people remaining
in town—the last legacy of capitalist enterprise. They became free while we were
in Petersburg. Previously there had been
a charge of two or three roubles—the
hundredth part of the price of an egg.
Freeing them made little difference in
their extreme congestion during the home-
going hours. Every one scrambles on the
tramcar. If there is no room inside you
cluster outside. In the busy hours festoons
of people hang outside by any handhold ;
people are frequently pushed off, and
accidents are frequent. We saw a crowd
collected round a child cut in half by
a tramcar, and two people in the little

circle in which we moved in Petersburg had broken their legs in tramway accidents.

The roads along which these tramcars run are in a frightful condition. They have not been repaired for three or four years ; they are full of holes like shell-holes, often two or three feet deep. Frost has eaten out great cavities, drains have collapsed, and people have torn up the wood pavement for fires. Only once did we see any attempt to repair the streets in Petrograd. In a side street some mysterious agency had collected a load of wood blocks and two barrels of tar. Most of our longer journeys about the town were done in official motor-cars—left over from the former times. A drive is an affair of tremendous swerves and concussions. These surviving motor-cars are running now on kerosene. They disengage clouds of pale blue smoke, and start up with a noise like a machine-gun battle. Every wooden house was demolished for firing last winter, and such masonry as there was in those houses remains in ruinous gaps, between the houses of stone.

Every one is shabby ; every one seems to be carrying bundles in both Petersburg and Moscow. To walk into some side street in the twilight and see nothing but ill-clad figures, all hurrying, all carrying loads, gives one an impression as though the entire population was setting out in flight. That impression is not altogether misleading. The Bolshevik statistics I have seen are perfectly frank and honest in the matter. The population of Petersburg has fallen from 1,200,000 (before 1919) to a little over 700,000, and it is still falling. Many people have returned to peasant life in the country, many have gone abroad, but hardship has taken an enormous toll of this city. The death-rate in Petersburg is over 81 per 1,000 ; formerly it was high among European cities at 22. The birth-rate of the underfed and profoundly depressed population is about 15. It was formerly about 30.

These bundles that every one carries

C

are partly the rations of food that are doled
out by the Soviet organisation, partly they
are the material and results of illicit trade.
The Russian population has always been
a trading and bargaining population. Even
in 1914 there were but few shops in Petersburg whose prices were really fixed prices.
Tariffs were abominated ; in Moscow
taking a droshky meant always a haggle,
ten kopecks at a time. Confronted with
a shortage of nearly every commodity, a
shortage caused partly by the war strain,—
for Russia has been at war continuously
now for six years—partly by the general
collapse of social organisation, and partly
by the blockade, and with a currency in
complete disorder, the only possible way
to save the towns from a chaos of cornering,
profiteering, starvation, and at last a mere
savage fight for the remnants of food and
common necessities, was some sort of
collective control and rationing.

The Soviet Government rations on principle, but any Government in Russia now
would have to ration.   If the war in the

West had lasted up to the present time
London would be rationing too—food,
clothing, and housing. But in Russia
this has to be done on a basis of uncon-
trollable peasant production, with a population temperamentally indisciplined and
self-indulgent. The struggle is necessarily
a bitter one. The detected profiteer, the
genuine profiteer who profiteers on any
considerable scale, gets short shrift; he
is shot. Quite ordinary trading may be
punished severely. All trading is called
" speculation," and is now illegal. But a
queer street-corner trading in food and so
forth is winked at in Petersburg, and quite
openly practised in Moscow, because only
by permitting this can the peasants be
induced to bring in food.

There is also much underground trade
between buyers and sellers who know each
other. Every one who can supplements
his public rations in this way. And every
railway station at which one stops is an
open market. We would find a crowd of
peasants at every stopping-place waiting

to sell milk, eggs, apples, bread, and so forth. The passengers clamber down and accumulate bundles. An egg or an apple costs 300 roubles.

The peasants look well fed, and I doubt if they are very much worse off than they were in 1914. Probably they are better off. They have more land than they had, and they have got rid of their landlords. They will not help in any attempt to overthrow the Soviet Government because they are convinced that while it endures this state of things will continue. This does not prevent their resisting whenever they can the attempts of the Red Guards to collect food at regulation prices. Insufficient forces of Red Guards may be attacked and massacred. Such incidents are magnified in the London Press as peasant insurrections against the Bolsheviks. They are nothing of the sort. It is just the peasants making themselves comfortable under the existing *régime*.

But every class above the peasants—including the official class—is now in a

state of extreme privation. The credit
and industrial system that produced com-
modities has broken down, and so far the
attempts to replace it by some other form
of production have been ineffective. So
that nowhere are there any new things.
About the only things that seem to be
fairly well supplied are tea, cigarettes, and
matches. Matches are more abundant in
Russia than they were in England in 1917,
and the Soviet State match is quite a good
match. But such things as collars, ties,
shoelaces, sheets and blankets, spoons and
forks, all the haberdashery and crockery of
life, are unattainable. There is no replacing a broken cup or glass except by a
sedulous search and illegal trading. From
Petersburg to Moscow we were given a
sleeping car de luxe, but there were no
water-bottles, glasses, or, indeed, any loose
fittings. They have all gone. Most of
the men one meets strike one at first as
being carelessly shaven, and at first we
were inclined to regard that a a sign of a
general apathy, but we underst od better

how things were when a friend mentioned
to my son quite casually that he had been
using one safety razor blade for nearly a
year.

Drugs and any medicines are equally
unattainable. There is nothing to take
for a cold or a headache ; no packing off
to bed with a hot-water bottle. Small
ailments develop very easily therefore into
serious trouble. Nearly everybody we met
struck us as being uncomfortable and a
little out of health. A buoyant, healthy
person is very rare in this atmosphere of
discomforts and petty deficiencies.

If any one falls into a real illness the
outlook is grim. My son paid a visit to
the big Obuchovskaya Hospital, and he
tells me things were very miserable there
indeed. There was an appalling lack of
every sort of material, and half the beds
were not in use through the sheer impos-
sibility of dealing with more patients if
they came in   Strengthening and stimu-
lating food is out of the question unless the
patient's family can by some miracle

procure it outside and send it in. Operations are performed only on one day in the
week, Dr. Federoff told me, when the
necessary preparations can be made. On
other days they are impossible, and the
patient must wait.

Hardly any one in Petersburg has much
more than a change of raiment, and in a
great city in which there remains no
means of communication but a few overcrowded tramcars,* old, leaky, and ill-
fitting boots are the only footwear. At
times one sees astonishing makeshifts by
way of costume. The master of a school
to which we paid a surprise visit struck me
as unusually dapper. He was wearing a
dinner suit with a blue serge waistcoat.
Several of the distinguished scientific and
literary men I met had no collars and wore
neck-wraps. Gorky possesses only the
one suit of clothes he wears.

At a gathering of literary people in

* I saw one passenger steamboat on the Neva
crowded with passengers. Usually the river was
quite deserted except for a rare Government tug or
a solitary boatman picking up drift timber.

Petersburg, Mr. Amphiteatroff, the well-
known writer, addressed a long and bitter
speech to me. He suffered from the usual
delusion that I was blind and stupid and
being hoodwinked. He was for taking off
the respectable-looking coats of all the
company present in order that I might see
for myself the rags and tatters and pitiful
expedients beneath. It was a painful and,
so far as I was concerned, an unnecessary
speech, but I quote it here to emphasise
this effect of general destitution. And this
underclad town population in this dis-
mantled and ruinous city is, in spite of all
the furtive trading that goes on, appallingly
underfed. With the best will in the world
the Soviet Government is unable to produce a sufficient ration to sustain a healthy
life. We went to a district kitchen and
saw the normal food distribution going on.
The place seemed to us fairly clean and
fairly well run, but that does not com-
pensate for a lack of material. The lowest
grade ration consisted of a basinful of thin
skilly and about the same quantity of

STREET SCENERY IN PETERSBURG.

MR. WELLS DISCOVERS A STREET UNDER REPAIR.

stewed apple compote. People have bread cards and wait in queues for bread, but for three days the Petersburg bakeries stopped for lack of flour. The bread varies greatly in quality ; some was good coarse brown bread, and some I found damp, clay-like, and uneatable.

I do not know how far these disconnected details will suffice to give the Western reader an idea of what ordinary life in Petersburg is at the present time. Moscow, they say, is more overcrowded and shorter of fuel than Petersburg, but superficially it looked far less grim than Petersburg. We saw these things in October, in a particularly fine and warm October. We saw them in sunshine in a setting of ruddy and golden foliage. But one day there came a chill, and the yellow leaves went whirling before a drive of snowflakes. It was the first breath of the coming winter. Every one shivered and looked out of the double windows—already sealed up—and talked to us of the previous year. Then the glow of October returned.

It was still glorious sunshine when we left Russia. But when I think of that coming winter my heart sinks. The Soviet Government in the commune of the north has made extraordinary efforts to prepare for the time of need. There are piles of wood along the quays, along the middle of the main streets, in the courtyards, and in every place where wood can be piled. Last year many people had to live in rooms below the freezing point ; the water-pipes froze up, the sanitary machinery ceased to work. The reader must imagine the consequences. People huddled together in the ill-lit rooms, and kept themselves alive with tea and talk. Presently some Russian novelist will tell us all that this has meant to heart and mind in Russia. This year it may not be quite so bad as that. The food situation also, they say, is better, but this I very much doubt. The railways are now in an extreme state of deterioration ; the wood-stoked engines are wearing out ; the bolts start and the rails shift as the trains rumble along at a maximum of

twenty-five miles per hour. Even were
the railways more efficient, Wrangel has
got hold of the southern food supplies.
Soon the cold rain will be falling upon
these 700,000 souls still left in Petersburg,
and then the snow. The long nights
extend and the daylight dwindles.

And this spectacle of misery and ebbing
energy is, you will say, the result of
Bolshevist rule ! I do not believe it is.
I will deal with the Bolshevist Government
when I have painted the general scenery of
our problem. But let me say here that
this desolate Russia is not a system that
has been attacked and destroyed by something vigorous and malignant. It is an
unsound system that has worked itself out
and fallen down. It was not communism
which built up these great, impossible
cities, but capitalism. It was not communism that plunged this huge, creaking,
bankrupt empire into six years of exhaust-
ing war. It was European imperialism.
Nor is it communism that has pestered this
suffering and perhaps dying Russia with a

series of subsidised raids, invasions, and insurrections, and inflicted upon it an atrocious blockade.   The vindictive French creditor, the journalistic British oaf, are far more responsible for these deathbed miseries than any communist. But to these questions I will return after I have given a little more description of Russia as we saw it during our visit.   It is only when one has some conception of the physical and mental realities of the Russian collapse that one can see and estimate the Bolshevist Government in its proper proportions.

II. *Drift and Salvage*

AMONG the things I wanted most to see amid this tremendous spectacle of social collapse in Russia was the work of my old friend Maxim Gorky. I had heard of this from members of the returning labour delegation, and what they told me had whetted my desire for a closer view of what was going on. Mr. Bertrand Russell's description of Gorky's health had also made me anxious on his own account ; but I am happy to say that upon that score my news is good. Gorky seems as strong and well to me now as he was when I knew him first in 1906. And as a personality he has grown immensely. Mr. Russell wrote that Gorky is dying and that perhaps culture in Russia is dying too. Mr. Russell was, I think, betrayed by the artistic temptation of a dark and purple concluding passage. He found Gorky in bed and afflicted by a fit of coughing, and his imagination made the most of it.

Gorky's position in Russia is a quite extraordinary and personal one. He is no more of a communist than I am, and I have heard him argue with the utmost freedom in his flat against the extremist positions with such men as Bokaiev, recently the head of the Extraordinary Commission in Petersburg, and Zalutsky, one of the rising leaders of the Communist party. It was a very reassuring display of free speech, for Gorky did not so much argue as denounce—and this in front of two deeply interested English enquirers.

But he has gained the confidence and respect of most of the Bolshevik leaders, and he has become by a kind of necessity the semi-official salvage man under the new *régime*. He is possessed by a passionate sense of the value of Western science and culture, and by the necessity of preserving the intellectual continuity of Russian life through these dark years of famine and war and social stress, with the general intellectual life of the world. He has found a steady supporter in Lenin. His work illuminates the situation to an extraordinary degree because it collects together a number of significant factors and makes the essentially catastrophic nature of the Russian situation plain.

The Russian smash at the end of 1917 was certainly the completest that has ever happened to any modern social organisation. After the failure of the Kerensky Government to make peace and of the British naval authorities to relieve the situation upon the Baltic flank, the shattered Russian armies, weapons in hand, broke up and rolled back upon Russia, a flood of peasant soldiers making for home, without hope, without supplies, without discipline. That time of *débâcle* was a time of complete social disorder. It was a social dissolution. In many parts of Russia there was a peasant revolt. There was château-burning, often accompanied by quite horrible atrocities. It was an explosion of the very worst side of human

D

nature in despair, and for most of the abominations committed the Bolsheviks are about as responsible as the Government of Australia. People would be held up and robbed even to their shirts in open daylight in the streets of Petersburg and Moscow, no one interfering. Murdered bodies lay disregarded in the gutters sometimes for a whole day, with passengers on the footwalk going to and fro. Armed men, often professing to be Red Guards, entered houses and looted and murdered. The early months of 1918 saw a violent struggle of the new Bolshevik Government not only with counter-revolutions but with robbers and brigands of every description. It was not until the summer of 1918, and after thousands of looters and plunderers had been shot, that life began to be ordinarily safe again in the streets of the Russian great towns. For a time Russia was not a civilisation, but a torrent of lawless violence, with a weak central Government of inexperienced rulers, fighting not only against unintelligent foreign intervention but against the completest internal disorder. It is from such chaotic conditions that Russia still struggles to emerge.

Art, literature, science, all the refinements and elaboration of life, all that we mean by " civilisation," were involved in this torrential catastrophe. For a time the stablest thing in Russian culture was the theatre. There stood the theatres, and nobody wanted to loot them or destroy them ; the artists were accustomed to meet and work in them and went on meeting and working ; the tradition of official subsidies held good. So quite amazingly the Russian dramatic and operatic life kept on through the extremest stormsof violence, and keeps on to this day. In Petersburg we found there were more than forty shows going on every night ; in Moscow we found very much the same state of affairs. We heard Shalyapin, greatest of actors and singers, in *The Barber of Seville* and in *Chovanchina ;* the admirable orchestra was variously attired, but the conductor still

held out valiantly in swallow tails and a
white tie ; we saw a performance of *Sadko*,
we saw Monachof in *The Tsarevitch Alexei*
and as Iago in *Othello* (with Madame
Gorky—Madame Andreievna—as Desde-
mona). When one faced the stage, it was
as if nothing had changed in Russia ; but
when the curtain fell and one turned to the
audience one realised the revolution. There
were now no brilliant uniforms, no evening
dress in boxes and stalls. The audience was
an undifferentiated mass of people, the same
sort of people everywhere, attentive, good-
humoured, well-behaved and shabby. Like
the London Stage Society, one's place in
the house is determined by ballot. And
for the most part there is no paying to
enter the theatre. For one performance the
tickets go, let us say, to the professional
unions, for another to the Red Army and
their families, for another to the school
children, and so on. A certain selling of
tickets goes on, but it is not in the present
scheme of things.

I had heard Shalyapin in London, but

I had not met him personally there. We
made his acquaintance this time in Petersburg, we dined with him and saw something
of his very jolly household. There are
two stepchildren almost grown up, and
two little daughters, who speak a nice,
stiff, correct English, and the youngest of
whom dances delightfully. Shalyapin is
certainly one of the most wonderful things
in Russia at the present time. He is the
Artist, defiant and magnificent. Off the
stage he has much the same vitality and
abounding humour that made an encounter
with Beerbohm Tree so delightful an
experience. He refuses absolutely to sing
except for pay—200,000 roubles a performance, they say, which is nearly £15—
and when the markets get too tight, he
insists upon payment in flour or eggs or the
like. What he demands he gets, for
Shalyapin on strike would leave too dismal
a hole altogether in the theatrical world of
Petersburg. So it is that he maintains
what is perhaps the last fairly comfortable
home in Russia. And Madame Shalyapin

we found so unbroken by the revolution
that she asked us what people were wearing
in London. The last fashion papers she
had seen—thanks to the blockade—dated
from somewhen early in 1918.

But the position of the theatre among the
arts is peculiar. For the rest of the arts,
for literature generally and for the scientific
worker, the catastrophe of 1917–18 was
overwhelming. There remained no one
to buy books or pictures, and the scientific
worker found himself with a salary of
roubles that dwindled rapidly to less than
the five-hundredth part of their original
value. The new crude social organisation,
fighting robbery, murder, and the wildest
disorder, had no place for them ; it had
forgotten them. For the scientific men at
first the Soviet Government had as little
regard as the first French revolution, which
had " no need for chemists." These
classes of worker, vitally important to
every civilised system, were reduced, therefore, to a state of the utmost privation and
misery. It was to their assistance and

salvation that Gorky's first efforts were directed. Thanks very largely to him and to the more creative intelligences in the Bolshevik Government, there has now been organised a group of salvage establishments, of which the best and most fully developed is the House of Science in Petersburg, in the ancient palace of the Archduchess Marie Pavlova. Here we saw the headquarters of a special rationing system which provides as well as it can for the needs of four thousand scientific workers and their dependants—in all perhaps for ten thousand people. At this centre they not only draw their food rations, but they can get baths and barber, tailoring, cobbling and the like conveniences. There is even a small stock of boots and clothing. There are bedrooms, and a sort of hospital accommodation for cases of weakness and ill-health.

It was to me one of the strangest of my Russian experiences to go to this institution and to meet there, as careworn and unprosperous-looking figures, some of the great survivors of the Russian scientific world. Here were such men as Oldenburg the orientalist, Karpinsky the geologist, Pavloff the Nobel prizeman, Radloff, Bielopolsky, and the like, names of world-wide celebrity. They asked me a multitude of questions about recent scientific progress in the world outside Russia, and made me ashamed of my frightful ignorance of such matters. If I had known that this would happen I would have taken some sort of report with me. Our blockade has cut them off from all scientific literature outside Russia. They are without new instruments, they are short of paper, the work they do has to go on in unwarmed laboratories. It is amazing they do any work at all. Yet they are getting work done ; Pavloff is carrying on research of astonishing scope and ingenuity upon the mentality of animals ; Manuchin claims to have worked out an effectual cure for tuberculosis, even in advanced cases ; and so on. I have brought back abstracts of Manuchin's work for translation and publication here,

A Petersburg Street Car en Route.

Messrs. Lenin and Wells in Conversation.

and they are now being put into English. The scientific spirit is a wonderful spirit. If Petersburg starves this winter, the House of Science—unless we make some special effort on its behalf—will starve too, but these scientific men said very little to me about the possibility of sending them in supplies. The House of Literature and Art talked a little of want and miseries, but not the scientific men. What they were all keen about was the possibility of getting scientific publications ; they value knowledge more than bread. Upon that matter I hope I may be of some help to them. I got them to form a committee to make me out a list of all the books and publications of which they stood in need, and I have brought this list back to the Secretary of the Royal Society of London, which had already been stirring in this matter. Funds will be needed, three or four thousand pounds perhaps (the address of the Secretary of the Royal Society is Burlington House, W.), but the assent of the Bolshevik Government and our own to this mental provisioning of Russia has been secured, and in a little time I hope the first parcel of books will be going through to these men, who have been cut off for so long from the general mental life of the world.

If I had no other reason for satisfaction about this trip to Russia, I should find quite enough in the hope and comfort our mere presence evidently gave to many of these distinguished men in the House of Science and in the House of Literature and Art. Upon many of them there had settled a kind of despair of ever seeing or hearing anything of the outer world again. They had been living for three years, very grey and long years indeed, in a world that seemed sinking down steadily through one degree of privation after another into utter darkness. Possibly they had seen something of one or two of the political deputations that have visited Russia—I do not know ; but manifestly they had never expected to see again a free and independent individual

walk in, with an air of having come quite
easily and unofficially from London, and
of its being quite possible not only to come
but to go again into the lost world of the
West. It was like an unexpected afternoon
caller strolling into a cell in a gaol.

All musical people in England know the
work of Glazounov ; he has conducted
concerts in London and is an honorary
doctor both of Oxford and Cambridge.
I was very deeply touched by my meeting
with him. He used to be a big florid
man, but now he is pallid and much
fallen away, so that his clothes hang loosely
on him. He came and talked of his friends
Sir Hubert Parry and Sir Charles Villiers
Stanford. He told me he still composed,
but that his stock of music paper was
almost exhausted. " Then there will be
no more." I said there would be much
more, and that soon. He doubted it. He
spoke of London and Oxford ; I could see
that he was consumed by an almost
intolerable longing for some great city
full of life, a city with abundance, with

pleasant crowds, a city that would give him stirring audiences in warm, brightly-lit places. While I was there, I was a sort of living token to him that such things could still be. He turned his back on the window which gave on the cold grey Neva, deserted in the twilight, and the low lines of the fortress prison of St. Peter and St. Paul. " In England there will be no revolution—no ? I had many friends in England—many good friends in England. . . ." I was loth to leave him, and he was very loth to let me go.

Seeing all these distinguished men living a sort of refugee life amidst the impoverished ruins of the fallen imperialist system has made me realise how helplessly dependent the man of exceptional gifts is upon a securely organised civilisation. The ordinary man can turn from this to that occupation ; he can be a sailor or a worker in a factory or a digger or what not. He is under a general necessity to work, but he has no internal demon which compels him to do a particular thing and nothing else, which compels him to be a particular thing or die. But a Shalyapin must be Shalyapin or nothing, Pavloff is Pavloff and Glazounov, Glazounov. So long as they can go on doing their particular thing, such men will live and flourish. Shalyapin still acts and sings magnificently—in absolute defiance of every Communist principle ; Pavloff still continues his marvellous researches— in an old coat and with his study piled up with the potatoes and carrots he grows in his spare time ; Glazounov will compose until the paper runs out. But many of the others are evidently stricken much harder. The mortality among the intellectually distinguished men of Russia has been terribly high. Much, no doubt, has been due to the general hardship of life, but in many cases I believe that the sheer mortification of great gifts become futile has been the determining cause. They could no more live in the Russia of 1919 than they could have lived in a Kaffir kraal.

Science, art, and literature are hothouse plants demanding warmth and respect and service. It is the paradox of science that it alters the whole world and is produced by the genius of men who need protection and help more than any other class of worker. The collapse of the Russian imperial system has smashed up all the shelters in which such things could exist. The crude Marxist philosophy which divides all men into bourgeoisie and pro-letariat, which sees all social life as a stupidly simple " class war," had no knowledge of the conditions necessary for the collective mental life. But it is to the credit of the Bolshevik Government that it has now risen to the danger of a universal intellectual destruction in Russia, and that, in spite of the blockade and the unending struggle against the subsidised revolts and invasions with which we and the French plague Russia, it is now per-mitting and helping these salvage organisa-tions. Parallel with the House of Science is the House of Literature and Art. The writing of new books, except for some poetry, and the painting of pictures have ceased in Russia. But the bulk of the writers and artists have been found employment upon a grandiose scheme for the publication of a sort of Russian encyclopædia of the literature of the world. In this strange Russia of conflict, cold, famine and pitiful privations there is actually going on now a literary task that would be inconceivable in the rich England and the rich America of to-day. In England and America the production of good literature at popular prices has practically ceased now—" because of the price of paper." The mental food of the English and American masses dwindles and deteriorates, and nobody in authority cares a rap. The Bolshevik Government is at least a shade above that level. In starving Russia hundreds of people are working upon translations, and the books they translate are being set up and printed, work which may presently give a new Russia such a knowledge of world thought as no other people will possess. I have seen some of the books and the work going on. " May " I write, with no certainty. Because, like everything else in this ruined country, this creative work is essentially improvised and fragmentary. How this world literature is to be distributed to the Russian people I do not know. The book-shops are closed and bookselling, like every other form of trading, is illegal. Probably the books will be distributed to schools and other institutions.

In this matter of book distribution the Bolshevik authorities are clearly at a loss. They are at a loss upon very many such matters. In regard to the intellectual life of the community one discovers that Marxist Communism is without plans and without ideas. Marxist Communism has always been a theory of revolution, a theory not merely lacking in creative and constructive ideas, but hostile to creative and constructive ideas. Every Communist orator has been trained to contemn " Utopianism," that is to say, has been

GORKY IN THE GREAT DUMP OF ART AND VIRTUOSITY IN
PETERSBURG.

trained to contemn intelligent planning. Not even a British business man of the older type is quite such a believer in things righting themselves and in " muddling through " as these Marxists. The Russian Communist Government now finds itself face to face, among a multiplicity of other constructive problems, with the problem of sustaining scientific life, of sustaining thought and discussion, of promoting artistic creation. Marx the Prophet and his Sacred Book supply it with no lead at all in the matter. Bolshevism, having no schemes, must improvise therefore—clumsily, and is reduced to these pathetic attempts to salvage the wreckage of the intellectual life of the old order. And that life is very sick and unhappy and seems likely to die on its hands.

It is not simply scientific and literary work and workers that Maxim Gorky is trying to salvage in Russia. There is a third and still more curious salvage organisation associated with him. This is the Expertise Commission, which has its head-

E

quarters in the former British Embassy.
When a social order based on private
property crashes, when private property
is with some abruptness and no qualifica-
tion abolished, this does not abolish and
destroy the things which have hitherto
constituted private property. Houses and
their gear remain standing, still being
occupied and used by the people who had
them before—except when those people
have fled. When the Bolshevik authorities
requisition a house or take over a deserted
palace, they find themselves faced by this
problem of the gear. Any one who knows
human nature will understand that there
has been a certain amount of quiet annexa-
tion of desirable things by inadvertent
officials and, perhaps less inadvertently, by
their wives. But the general spirit of
Bolshevism is quite honest, and it is set
very stoutly against looting and suchlike
developments of individual enterprise.
There has evidently been comparatively
little looting either in Petersburg or Moscow
since the days of the *débâcle*. Looting died

against the wall in Moscow in the spring of
1918. In the guest houses and suchlike
places we noted that everything was
numbered and listed. Occasionally we
saw odd things astray, fine glass or crested
silver upon tables where it seemed out of
place, but in many cases these were things
which had been sold for food or suchlike
necessities on the part of the original
owners. The sailor courier who attended
to our comfort to and from Moscow was
provided with a beautiful little silver teapot
that must once have brightened a charming
drawing-room. But apparently it had
taken to a semi-public life in a quite
legitimate way.

For greater security there has been a
gathering together and a cataloguing of
everything that could claim to be a work
of art by this Expertise Commission.
The palace that once sheltered the British
Embassy is now like some congested
second-hand art shop in the Brompton
Road. We went through room after room
piled with the beautiful lumber of the

E 2

former Russian social system. There are
big rooms crammed with statuary; never
have I seen so many white marble Venuses
and sylphs together, not even in the
Naples Museum. There are stacks of
pictures of every sort, passages choked
with inlaid cabinets piled up to the ceiling;
a room full of cases of old lace, piles of
magnificent furniture. This accumulation
has been counted and catalogued. And
there it is. I could not find out that any
one had an idea of what was ultimately
to be done with all this lovely and elegant
litter. The stuff does not seem to belong
in any way to the new world, if it is indeed
a new world that the Russian Communists
are organising. They never anticipated
that they would have to deal with such
things. Just as they never really thought
of what they would do with the shops and
markets when they had abolished shopping
and marketing. Just as they had never
thought out the problem of converting a
city of private palaces into a Communist
gathering-place. Marxist theory had led

their minds up to the " dictatorship of the
class-conscious proletariat " and then inti-
mated—we discover now how vaguely—
that there would be a new heaven and a
new earth. Had that happened it would
indeed have been a revolution in human
affairs. But as we saw Russia there is
still the old heaven and the old earth,
covered with the ruins, littered with the
abandoned furnishings and dislocated machinery of the former system, with the old
peasant tough and obstinate upon the soil
—and Communism, ruling in the cities
quite pluckily and honestly, and yet, in
so many matters, like a conjurer who has
left his pigeon and his rabbit behind him,
and can produce nothing whatever from
the hat.

Ruin ; that is the primary Russian fact
at the present time. The revolution, the
Communist rule, which I will proceed to
describe in my next paper, is quite secondary to that. It is something that has
happened in the ruin and because of the
ruin. It is of primary importance that

people in the West should realise that. If
the Great War had gone on for a year or
so more, Germany and then the Western
Powers would probably have repeated, with
local variations, the Russian crash. The
state of affairs we have seen in Russia is
only the intensification and completion of
the state of affairs towards which Britain
was drifting in 1918. Here also there are
shortages such as we had in England, but
they are relatively monstrous ; here also
is rationing, but it is relatively feeble and
inefficient ; the profiteer in Russia is not
fined but shot, and for the English
D.O.R.A. you have the Extraordinary
Commission. What were nuisances in
England are magnified to disasters in
Russia. That is all the difference. For
all I know, Western Europe may be still
drifting even now towards a parallel crash.
I am not by any means sure that we have
turned the corner. War, self-indulgence,
and unproductive speculation may still be
wasting more than the Western world is
producing ; in which case our own crash—

currency failure, a universal shortage, social and political collapse and all the rest of it—is merely a question of time. The shops of Regent Street will follow the shops of the Nevsky Prospect, and Mr. Galsworthy and Mr. Bennett will have to do what they can to salvage the art treasures of Mayfair. It falsifies the whole world situation, it sets people altogether astray in their political actions, to assert that the frightful destitution of Russia to-day is to any large extent the result merely of Communist effort ; that the wicked Communists have pulled down Russia to her present plight, and that if you can overthrow the Communists every one and everything in Russia will suddenly become happy again. Russia fell into its present miseries through the world war and the moral and intellectual insufficiency of its ruling and wealthy people. (As our own British State—as presently even the American State—may fall.) They had neither the brains nor the conscience to stop warfare, stop waste of all sorts, and stop taking the best of every-

thing and leaving every one else dangerously
unhappy, until it was too late. They ruled
and wasted and quarrelled, blind to the
coming disaster up to the very moment of
its occurrence. And then, as I describe
in the next chapters, the Communist
came in. . . .

III. The Quintessence of Bolshevism

IN the two preceding chapters I have tried
to give the reader my impression of
Russian life as I saw it in Petersburg and
Moscow, as a spectacle of collapse, as the
collapse of a political, social, and economic
system, akin to our own but weaker and
more rotten than our own, which has
crashed under the pressure of six years of
war and misgovernment. The main collapse occurred in 1917 when Tsarism,
brutishly incompetent, became manifestly
impossible. It had wasted the whole
land, lost control of its army and the
confidence of the entire population. Its
police system had degenerated into a
régime of violence and brigandage. It
fell inevitably.

And there was no alternative government. For generations the chief energies
of Tsarism had been directed to destroying

any possibility of an alternative government. It had subsisted on that one fact
that, bad as it was, there was nothing else
to put in its place. The first Russian
Revolution, therefore, turned Russia into
a debating society and a political scramble.
The liberal forces of the country, un-
accustomed to action or responsibility, set
up a clamorous discussion whether Russia
was to be a constitutional monarchy, a
liberal republic, a socialist republic, or
what not. Over the confusion gesticulated
Kerensky in attitudes of the finest liberal-
ism. Through it loomed various ambiguous
adventurers, " strong men," sham strong
men, Russian Monks and Russian Bona-
partes. What remained of social order
collapsed. In the closing months of 1917
murder and robbery were common street
incidents in Petersburg and Moscow, as
common as an automobile accident in the
streets of London, and less heeded. On
the Reval boat was an American who had
formerly directed the affairs of the American Harvester Company in Russia. He

THE STATUE OF MARX OUTSIDE THE SMOLNY INSTITUTE.
(Headquarters of the Communist Party.)

had been in Moscow during this phase of
complete disorder. He described hold-ups
in open daylight in busy streets, dead
bodies lying for hours in the gutter—as a
dead kitten might do in a western town—
while crowds went about their business
along the side-walk.

Through this fevered and confused
country went the representatives of Britain
and France, blind to the quality of the
immense and tragic disaster about them,
intent only upon *the* war, badgering the
Russians to keep on fighting and make a
fresh offensive against Germany. But
when the Germans made a strong thrust
towards Petersburg through the Baltic
provinces and by sea, the British Admiralty,
either through sheer cowardice or through
Royalist intrigues, failed to give any effectual help to Russia. Upon this matter the
evidence of the late Lord Fisher is plain.
And so this unhappy country, mortally
sick and, as it were, delirious, staggered
towards a further stage of collapse.

From end to end of Russia, and in the

Russian-speaking community throughout the world, there existed only one sort of people who had common general ideas upon which to work, a common faith and a common will, and that was the Communist party. While all the rest of Russia was either apathetic like the peasantry or garrulously at sixes and sevens or given over to violence or fear, the Communists believed and were prepared to act. Numerically they were and are a very small part of the Russian population. At the present time not one per cent. of the people in Russia are Communists ; the organised party certainly does not number more than 600,000 and has probably not much more than 150,000 active members. Nevertheless, because it was in those terrible days the only organisation which gave men a common idea of action, common formulæ, and mutual confidence, it was able to seize and retain control of the smashed empire. It was and it is the only sort of administrative solidarity possible in Russia. These ambiguous adventurers

who have been and are afflicting Russia,
with the support of the Western Powers,
Deniken, Kolchak, Wrangel and the like,
stand for no guiding principle and offer no
security of any sort upon which men's
confidence can crystallise. They are
essentially brigands. The Communist
party, however one may criticise it, does
embody an idea and can be relied upon to
stand by its idea. So far it is a thing
morally higher than anything that has yet
come against it. It at once secured the
passive support of the peasant mass by
permitting them to take land from the
estates and by making peace with Germany.
It restored order—after a frightful lot of
shooting—in the great towns. For a
time everybody found carrying arms without authority was shot. This action was
clumsy and bloody but effective. To
retain its power this Communist Government organised Extraordinary Commis-
sions, with practically unlimited powers,
and crushed out all opposition by a Red
Terror. Much that that Red Terror did

was cruel and frightful, it was largely controlled by narrow-minded men, and many of its officials were inspired by social hatred and the fear of counter-revolution, but if it was fanatical it was honest. Apart from individual atrocities it did on the whole kill for a reason and to an end. Its bloodshed was not like the silly aimless butcheries of the Deniken *régime*, which would not even recognise, I was told, the Bolshevik Red Cross. And to-day the Bolshevik Government sits, I believe, in Moscow as securely established as any Government in Europe, and the streets of the Russian towns are as safe as any streets in Europe.

It not only established itself and restored order, but—thanks largely to the genius of that ex-pacifist Trotsky—it re-created the Russian army as a fighting force. That we must recognise as a very remarkable achievement. I saw little of the Russian army myself, it was not what I went to Russia to see, but Mr. Vanderlip, the enterprising American financier, whom I found

PROLETARIANS OF ASIA A LA BAKU.

in Moscow engaged in some mysterious negotiations with the Soviet Government, had been treated to a review of several thousand troops, and was very enthusiastic about their spirit and equipment. My son and I saw a number of drafts going to the front, and also bodies of recruits joining up, and our impression is that the spirit of the men was quite as good as that of similar bodies of British recruits in London in 1917–18.

Now who are these Bolsheviki who have taken such an effectual hold upon Russia ? According to the crazier section of the British Press they are the agents of a mysterious racial plot, a secret society, in which Jews, Jesuits, Freemasons, and Germans are all jumbled together in the maddest fashion. As a matter of fact, nothing was ever quite less secret than the ideas and aims and methods of the Bolsheviks, nor anything quite less like a secret society than their organisation. But in England we cultivate a peculiar style of thinking, so impervious to any general

F

ideas that it must needs fall back upon the notion of a conspiracy to explain the simplest reactions of the human mind. If, for instance, a day labourer in Essex makes a fuss because he finds that the price of his children's boots has risen out of all proportion to the increase in his weekly wages, and declares that he and his fellow-workers are being cheated and underpaid, the editors of *The Times* and of the *Morning Post* will trace his resentment to the insidious propaganda of some mysterious society at Königsberg or Pekin. They cannot conceive how otherwise he should get such ideas into his head. Conspiracy mania of this kind is so prevalent that I feel constrained to apologise for my own immunity. I find the Bolsheviks very much what they profess to be. I find myself obliged to treat them as fairly straightforward people. I do not agree with either their views or their methods, but that is another question.

The Bolsheviks are Marxist Socialists. Marx died in London nearly forty years ago ; the propaganda of his views has been going on for over half a century. It has spread over the whole earth and finds in nearly every country a small but enthusiastic following. It is a natural result of world-wide economic conditions. Everywhere it expresses the same limited ideas in the same distinctive phrasing. It is a cult, a world-wide international brotherhood. No one need learn Russian to study the ideas of Bolshevism. The enquirer will find them all in the London *Plebs* or the New York *Liberator* in exactly the same phrases as in the Russian *Pravda*. They hide nothing. They say everything. And just precisely what these Marxists write and say, so they attempt to do.

It will be best if I write about Marx without any hypocritical deference. I have always regarded him as a Bore of the extremest sort. His vast unfinished work, *Das Kapital*, a cadence of wearisome volumes about such phantom unrealities as the *bourgeoisie* and the *proletariat*, a

F 2

book for ever maundering away into
tedious secondary discussions, impresses
me as a monument of pretentious pedantry.
But before I went to Russia on this last
occasion I had no active hostility to Marx.
I avoided his works, and when I encountered Marxists I disposed of them
by asking them to tell me exactly what
people constituted the proletariat. None
of them knew. No Marxist knows. In
Gorki's flat I listened with attention while
Bokaiev discussed with Shalyapin the fine
question of whether in Russia there was a
proletariat at all, distinguishable from the
peasants. As Bokaiev has been head of
the Extraordinary Commission of the Dictatorship of the Proletariat in Petersburg,
it was interesting to note the fine difficulties
of the argument. The " proletarian " in
the Marxist jargon is like the " producer "
in the jargon of some political economists,
who is supposed to be a creature absolutely
distinct and different from the " con-
sumer." So the proletarian is a figure
put into flat opposition to something called

capital. I find in large type outside the current number of the *Plebs*, " The working class and the employing class have nothing in common." Apply this to a works foreman who is being taken in a train by an engine-driver to see how the house he is having built for him by a building society is getting on. To which of these immiscibles does he belong, employer or employed ? The stuff is sheer nonsense.

In Russia I must confess my passive objection to Marx has changed to a very active hostility. Wherever we went we encountered busts, portraits, and statues of Marx. About two-thirds of the face of Marx is beard, a vast solemn woolly uneventful beard that must have made all normal exercise impossible. It is not the sort of beard that happens to a man, it is a beard cultivated, cherished, and thrust patriarchally upon the world. It is exactly like *Das Kapital* in its inane abundance, and the human part of the face looks over it owlishly as if it looked to see how the growth impressed mankind. I found the

omnipresent images of that beard more
and more irritating. A gnawing desire
grew upon me to see Karl Marx shaved.
Some day, if I am spared, I will take up
shears and a razor against *Das Kapital ;* I
will write *The Shaving of Karl Marx.*

But Marx is for the Marxists merely an
image and a symbol, and it is with the
Marxist and not with Marx that we are
now dealing. Few Marxists have read
much of *Das Kapital.* The Marxist is
very much the same sort of person in all
modern communities, and I will confess
that by my temperament and circumstances
I have the very warmest sympathy for
him. He adopts Marx as his prophet
simply because he believes that Marx
wrote of the class war, an implacable war
of the employed against the employer, and
that he prophesied a triumph for the
employed person, a dictatorship of the
world by the leaders of these liberated
employed persons (dictatorship of the
proletariat), and a Communist millennium
arising out of that dictatorship. Now this

doctrine and this prophecy have appealed
in every country with extraordinary power
to young persons, and particularly to
young men of energy and imagination who
have found themselves at the outset of
life imperfectly educated, ill-equipped, and
caught into hopeless wages slavery in our
existing economic system. They realise
in their own persons the social injustice,
the stupid negligence, the colossal incivility of our system ; they realise that
they are insulted and sacrificed by it ;
and they devote themselves to break it
and emancipate themselves from it. No
insidious propaganda is needed to make
such rebels ; it is the faults of a system
that half-educates and then enslaves them
which have created the Communist movement wherever industrialism has developed.
There would have been Marxists if Marx
had never lived. When I was a boy of
fourteen I was a complete Marxist, long
before I had heard the name of Marx. I
had been cut off abruptly from education,
caught in a detestable shop, and I was

being broken in to a life of mean and
dreary toil. I was worked too hard and
for such long hours that all thoughts of
self-improvement seemed hopeless. I
would have set fire to that place if I had
not been convinced it was over-insured.
I revived the spirit of those bitter days in
a conversation I had with Zorin, one of
the leaders of the Commune of the North.
He is a young man who has come back
from unskilled work in America, a very
likeable human being and a humorous and
very popular speaker in the Petersburg
Soviet. He and I exchanged experiences,
and I found that the thing that rankled
most in his mind about America was the
brutal incivility he had encountered when
applying for a job as packer in a big dry
goods store in New York. We told each
other stories of the way our social system
wastes and breaks and maddens decent
and willing men. Between us was the
freemasonry of a common indignation.

It is that indignation of youth and
energy, thwarted and misused, it is that

The Baku Conference Swears Undying Hostility to Capitalism and British Imperialism. Zenovieff (*by the bell*); to the right of him (*i.e.* on his left) are Radek (*spectacles*) and Bela Kun (*rather foggy*).

THE BAKU CONFERENCE SWEARS UNDYING HOSTILITY TO CAPITALISM AND BRITISH IMPERIALISM: THE BODY OF THE HALL.

and no mere economic theorising, which is the living and linking inspiration of the Marxist movement throughout the world. It is not that Marx was profoundly wise, but that our economic system has been stupid, selfish, wasteful, and anarchistic. The Communistic organisation has provided for this angry recalcitrance certain shibboleths and passwords ; " Workers of the World unite," and so forth. It has suggested to them an idea of a great conspiracy against human happiness concocted by a mysterious body of wicked men called capitalists. For in this mentally enfeebled world in which we live to-day conspiracy mania on one side finds its echo on the other, and it is hard to persuade a Marxist that capitalists are in their totality no more than a scrambling disorder of mean-spirited and short-sighted men. And the Communist propaganda has knitted all these angry and disinherited spirits together into a world-wide organisation of revolt—and hope—formless though that hope proves to be on examination. It has chosen Marx for its prophet and red for its colour. . . . And so when the crash came in Russia, when there remained no other solidarity of men who could work together upon any but immediate selfish ends, there came flowing back from America and the West to rejoin their comrades a considerable number of keen and enthusiastic young and youngish men, who had in that more bracing Western world lost something of the habitual impracticability of the Russian and acquired a certain habit of getting things done, who all thought in the same phrases and had the courage of the same ideas, and who were all inspired by the dream of a revolution that should bring human life to a new level of justice and happiness. It is these young men who constitute the living force of Bolshevism. Many of them are Jews, because most of the Russian emigrants to America were Jews ; but few of them have any strong racial Jewish feeling. They are not out for Jewry but for a new world. So far from being in continuation of the Jewish

tradition the Bolsheviks have put most of
the Zionist leaders in Russia in prison,
and they have proscribed the teaching of
Hebrew as a "reactionary" language.
Several of the most interesting Bolsheviks
I met were not Jews at all, but blond
Nordic men. Lenin, the beloved leader
of all that is energetic in Russia to-day,
has a Tartar type of face and is certainly
no Jew.

This Bolshevik Government is at once
the most temerarious and the least experienced governing body in the world. In
some directions its incompetence is amazing. In most its ignorance is profound.
Of the diabolical cunning of "capitalism"
and of the subtleties of reaction it is
ridiculously suspicious, and sometimes it
takes fright and is cruel. But essentially
it is honest. It is the most simple-minded
Government that exists in the world to-day.

Its simple-mindedness is shown by one
question that I was asked again and again
during this Russian visit. "When is the
social revolution going to happen in

England ? " Lenin asked me that, Zenovieff, who is the head of the Commune of
the North, Zorin, and many others.

Because it is by the Marxist theory all
wrong that the social revolution should
happen first in Russia. That fact is
bothering every intelligent man in the
movement. According to the Marxist
theory the social revolution should have
happened first in the country with the
oldest and most highly developed industrialism, with a large, definite, mainly
propertyless, mainly wages-earning working class (proletariat). It should have
begun in Britain, and spread to France and
Germany, then should have come America's
turn and so on. Instead they find Communism in power in Russia, which really
possesses no specialised labouring class at
all, which has worked its factories with
peasant labourers who come and go from
the villages, and so has scarcely any
" proletariat "—to unite with the workers
of the world and so forth—at all. Behind
the minds of many of these Bolsheviks with

whom I talked I saw clearly that there
dawns now a chill suspicion of the reality
of the case, a realisation that what they
have got in Russia is not truly the promised
Marxist social revolution at all, that in
truth they have not captured a State but
got aboard a derelict. I tried to assist the
development of this novel and disconcerting discovery. And also I indulged in a
little lecture on the absence of a large
" class-conscious proletariat " in the
Western communities. I explained that in
England there were two hundred different
classes at least, and that the only " class-
conscious proletarians " known to me in
the land were a small band of mainly
Scotch workers kept together by the
vigorous leadership of a gentleman named
MacManus. Their dearest convictions
struggled against my manifest candour.
They are clinging desperately to the belief
that there are hundreds of thousands of
convinced Communists in Britain, versed
in the whole gospel of Marx, a proletarian
solidarity, on the eve of seizing power and

proclaiming a British Soviet Republic.
They hold obstinately to that after three
years of waiting—but their hold weakens.

Among the most amusing things in this
queer intellectual situation are the repeated
scoldings that come by wireless from
Moscow to Western Labour because it
does not behave as Marx said it would
behave. It isn't red—and it ought to be.
It is just yellow.

My conversation with Zenovieff was
particularly curious. He is a man with
the voice and animation of Hilaire Belloc,
and a lot of curly coal-black hair. " You
have civil war in Ireland," he said.
" Practically," said I. " Which do you
consider are the proletarians, the Sinn
Feiners or the Ulstermen ? " We spent
some time while Zenovieff worked like a
man with a jigsaw puzzle trying to get
the Irish situation into the class war
formula. That jigsaw puzzle remained
unsolved, and we then shifted our attention
to Asia. Impatient at the long delay of
the Western proletarians to emerge and

declare themselves, Zenovieff, assisted by
Bela Kun, our Mr. Tom Quelch, and a
number of other leading Communists, has
recently gone on a pilgrimage to Baku to
raise the Asiatic proletariat. They went
to beat up the class-conscious wages slaves
of Persia and Turkestan. They sought out
factory workers and slum dwellers in the
tents of the steppes. They held a congress
at Baku, at which they gathered together
a quite wonderful accumulation of white,
black, brown, and yellow people, Asiatic
costumes and astonishing weapons. They
had a great assembly in which they swore
undying hatred of Capitalism and British
imperialism ; they had a great procession in
which I regret to say certain batteries of
British guns, which some careless, hasty
empire-builder had left behind him,
figured ; they disinterred and buried again
thirteen people whom this British empire-
builder seems to have shot without trial,
and they burnt Mr. Lloyd George, M.
Millerand, and President Wilson in effigy.
I not only saw a five-part film of this

remarkable festival when I visited the Petersburg Soviet, but, thanks to Zorin, I have brought the film back with me. It is to be administered with caution and to adults only. There are parts of it that would make Mr. Gwynne of the *Morning Post* or Mr. Rudyard Kipling scream in their sleep. If so be they ever slept again after seeing it.

I did my best to find out from Zenovieff and Zorin what they thought they were doing in the Baku Conference. And frankly I do not think they know. I doubt if they have anything clearer in their minds than a vague idea of hitting back at the British Government through Mesopotamia and India, because it has been hitting them through Kolchak, Deniken, Wrangel, and the Poles. It is a counter-offensive almost as clumsy and stupid as the offensives it would counter. It is inconceivable that they can hope for any social solidarity with the miscellaneous discontents their congress assembled. One item " featured " on this Baku film is a

dance by a gentleman from the neighbour-
hood of Baku. He is in fact one of the
main features of this remarkable film. He
wears a fur-trimmed jacket, high boots,
and a high cap, and his dancing is a very
rapid and dexterous step dancing. He
produces two knives and puts them between
his teeth, and then two others which he
balances perilously with the blades dangerously close to his nose on either side of it.
Finally he poises a fifth knife on his
forehead, still stepping it featly to the
distinctly Oriental music. He stoops and
squats, arms akimbo, sending his nimble
boots flying out and back like the Cossacks
in the Russian ballet. He circles slowly
as he does this, clapping his hands. He is
now rolled up in my keeping, ready to
dance again when opportunity offers. I
tried to find out whether he was a specimen
Asiatic proletarian or just what he sym-
bolised, but I could get no light on him.
But there are yards and yards of film of
him. I wish I could have resuscitated
Karl Marx, just to watch that solemn stare

G

over the beard, regarding him. The film
gives no indication of the dancer's reception
by Mr. Tom Quelch.

I hope I shall not offend Comrade Zorin,
for whom I have a real friendship, if I
thus confess to him that I cannot take his
Baku Conference very seriously. It was
an excursion, a pageant, a Beano. As a
meeting of Asiatic proletarians it was
preposterous. But if it was not very much
in itself, it was something very important
in its revelation of shifting intentions. Its
chief significance to me is this, that it
shows a new orientation of the Bolshevik
mind as it is embodied in Zenovieff. So
long as the Bolsheviki held firmly with
unshaken conviction to the Marxist formula
they looked westward, a little surprised
that the " social revolution " should have
begun so far to the east of its indicated
centre. Now as they begin to realise that
it is not that prescribed social revolution
at all but something quite different which
has brought them into power, they are
naturally enough casting about for a new

system of relationships. The ideal figure
of the Russian republic is still a huge
western " Worker," with a vast hammer or
a sickle. A time may come, if we maintain
the European blockade with sufficient
stringency and make any industrial
recuperation impossible, when that ideal
may give place altogether to a nomadic-
looking gentleman from Turkestan with a
number of knives. We may drive what
will remain of Bolshevik Russia to the
steppes and the knife. If we help some new
Wrangel to pull down the by no means
firmly established Government in Moscow,
under the delusion that thereby we shall
bring about " representative institutions "
and a " limited monarchy," we may find
ourselves very much out in our calculations.
Any one who destroys the present law and
order of Moscow will, I believe, destroy
what is left of law and order in Russia.
A brigand monarchist government will
leave a trail of fresh blood across the Russian scene, show what gentlemen can do
when they are roused, in a tremendous

G 2

pogrom and White Terror, flourish horribly for a time, break up and vanish. Asia will resume. The simple ancient rhythm of the horseman plundering the peasant and the peasant waylaying the horseman will creep back across the plains to the Niemen and the Dniester. The cities will become clusters of ruins in the waste ; the roads and railroads will rot and rust ; the river traffic will decay. . . .

This Baku Conference has depressed Gorky profoundly. He is obsessed by a nightmare of Russia going east. Perhaps I have caught a little of his depression.

IV.   *The Creative Effort in Russia*

IN the previous three chapters I have tried to give my impression of the Russian spectacle as that of a rather ramshackle modern civilisation completely shattered and overthrown by misgovernment, under-education, and finally six years of war strain. I have shown science and art starving and the comforts and many of the decencies of life gone. In Vienna the overthrow is just as bad ; and there too such men of science as the late Professor Margules starve to death. If London had had to endure four more years of war, much the same sort of thing would be happening in London. We should have now no coal in our grates and no food for our food tickets, and the shops in Bond Street would be as desolate as the shops in the Nevsky Prospect. Bolshevik government in Russia

is neither responsible for the causation nor
for the continuance of these miseries.

I have also tried to get the facts of
Bolshevik rule into what I believe is their
proper proportions in the picture. The
Bolsheviks, albeit numbering less than
five per cent. of the population, have been
able to seize and retain power in Russia
because they were and are the only body
of people in this vast spectacle of Russian
ruin with a common faith and a common
spirit. I disbelieve in their faith, I ridicule
Marx, their prophet, but I understand and
respect their spirit. They are—with all
their faults, and they have abundant faults
—the only possible backbone now to a
renascent Russia. The recivilising of
Russia must be done with the Soviet
Government as the starting phase. The
great mass of the Russian population is
an entirely illiterate peasantry, grossly
materialistic and politically indifferent.
They are superstitious, they are for ever
crossing themselves and kissing images,—
in Moscow particularly they were at it—

but they are not religious. They have no will in things political and social beyond their immediate satisfactions. They are roughly content with Bolshevik rule. The Orthodox priest is quite unlike the Catholic priest in Western Europe ; he is himself typically a dirty and illiterate peasant with no power over the wills and consciences of his people. There is no constructive quality in either peasant or Orthodoxy. For the rest there is a confusion of more or less civilised Russians, in and out of Russia, with no common political ideas and with no common will. They are incapable of producing anything but adventurers and disputes.

The Russian refugees in England are politically contemptible. They rehearse endless stories of " Bolshevik outrages " ; château-burnings by peasants, burglaries and murders by disbanded soldiers in the towns, back street crimes—they tell them all as acts of the Bolshevik Government. Ask them what government they want in its place, and you will get rubbishy

generalities—usually adapted to what the
speaker supposes to be your particular
political obsession. Or they sicken you
with the praise of some current super-man,
Deniken or Wrangel, who is to put everything right—God knows how. They
deserve nothing better than a Tsar, and
they are incapable even of deciding which
Tsar they desire. The better part of the
educated people still in Russia are—for the
sake of Russia—slowly drifting into a
reluctant but honest co-operation with
Bolshevik rule.

The Bolsheviks themselves are Marxists
and Communists. They find themselves
in control of Russia, in complete contra-
diction, as I have explained, to the theories
of Karl Marx. A large part of their
energies have been occupied in an entirely
patriotic struggle against the raids, invasions, blockades, and persecutions of every
sort that our insensate Western Governments
have rained upon their tragically s..attered
country. What is left over goes in the
attempt to keep Russia alive, and to

organise some sort of social order among the ruins. These Bolsheviks are, as I have explained, extremely inexperienced men, intellectual exiles from Geneva and Hampstead, or comparatively illiterate manual workers from the United States. Never was there so amateurish a government since the early Moslim found themselves in control of Cairo, Damascus, and Mesopotamia.

I believe that in the minds of very many of them there is a considerable element of dismay at the tremendous tasks they find before them. But one thing has helped them and Russia enormously, and that is their training in Communistic ideas. As the British found out during the submarine war, so far as the urban and industrial population goes there is nothing for it during a time of tragic scarcity but collapse or collective control. We in England had to control and ration, we had to suppress profiteering by stringent laws. These Communists came into power in Russia and began to do at once, on principle, the

first most necessary thing in that chaos of
social wreckage. Against all the habits
and traditions of Russia, they began to
control and ration—exhaustively. They
have now a rationing system that is, on
paper, admirable beyond cavil ; and perhaps it works as well as the temperament
and circumstances of Russian production
and consumption permit. It is easy to
note defects and failures, but not nearly
so easy to show how in this depleted and
demoralised Russia they could be avoided.
And things are in such a state in Russia
now that even if we suppose the Bolsheviks
overthrown and any other Government in
their place, it matters not what, that
Government would have to go on with the
rationing the Bolsheviks have organised,
with the suppression of vague political
experiments, and the punishment and
shooting of profiteers. The Bolsheviki in
this state of siege and famine have done
upon principle what any other Government
would have had to do from necessity.

And in the face of gigantic difficulties

they are trying to rebuild a new Russia among the ruins. We may quarrel with their principles and methods, we may call their schemes Utopian and so forth, we may sneer at or we may dread what they are doing, but it is no good pretending that there is no creative effort in Russia at the present time. A certain section of the Bolsheviks are hard-minded, doctrinaire and unteachable men, fanatics who believe that the mere destruction of capitalism, the disuse of money and trading, the effacement of all social differences, will in itself bring about a sort of bleak millennium. There are Bolsheviki so stupid that they would stop the teaching of chemistry in schools until they were assured it was " proletarian " chemistry, and who would suppress every decorative design that was not an elaboration of the letters R.S.F.S.R. (Russian Socialist Federal Soviet Republic) as reactionary art. I have told of the suppression of Hebrew studies because they are " reactionary " ; and while I was with Gorky I found him in constant bitter

disputes with extremist officials who would
see no good in any literature of the past
except the literature of revolt. But there
were other more liberal minds in this new
Russian world, minds which, given an
opportunity, will build and will probably
build well. Among men of such constructive force I would quote such names
as Lenin himself, who has developed
wonderfully since the days of his exile,
and who has recently written powerfully
against the extravagances of his own
extremists ; Trotsky, who has never been
an extremist, and who is a man of very
great organising ability ; Lunacharsky, the
Minister for Education ; Rikoff, the head
of the Department of People's Economy ;
Madame Lilna of the Petersburg Child
Welfare Department ; and Krassin, the
head of the London Trade Delegation.
These are names that occur to me ; it is
by no means an exhaustive list of the
statesmanlike elements in the Bolshevik
Government. Already they have achieved
something, in spite of blockade and civil

and foreign war. It is not only that they work to restore a country depleted of material to an extent almost inconceivable to English and American readers, but they work with an extraordinarily unhelpful personnel. Russia to-day stands more in need of men of the foreman and works-manager class than she does of medicaments or food. The ordinary work in the Government offices of Russia is shockingly done ; the slackness and inaccuracy are indescribable. Everybody seems to be working in a muddle of unsorted papers and cigarette ends. This again is a state of affairs no counter-revolution could change. It is inherent in the present Russian situation. If one of these military adventurers the Western Powers patronise were, by some disastrous accident, to get control of Russia, his success would only add strong drink, embezzlement, and a great squalour of kept mistresses to the general complication. For whatever else we may say to the discredit of the Bolshevik leaders, it is undeniable that the great

majority lead not simply laborious but
puritanical lives.

I write of this general inefficiency in
Russia with the more asperity because it
was the cause of my not meeting Lunacharsky. About eighty hours of my life
were consumed in travelling, telephoning,
and waiting about in order to talk for
about an hour and a half with Lenin and
for the same time with Tchitcherin. At
that rate, and in view of the intermittent
boat service from Reval to Stockholm, to
see Lunacharsky would have meant at
least a week more in Russia. The whole
of my visit to Moscow was muddled in the
most irritating fashion. A sailor-man carrying a silver kettle who did not know his
way about Moscow was put in charge of
my journey, and an American who did not
know enough Russian to telephone freely
was set to make my appointments in the
town. Although I had heard Gorky
arrange for my meeting with Lenin by
long - distance telephone days before,
Moscow declared that it had had no notice

of my coming. Finally I was put into the wrong train back to Petersburg, a train which took twenty-two hours instead of fourteen for the journey. These may seem petty details to relate, but when it is remembered that Russia was really doing its best to impress me with its vigour and good order, they are extremely significant. In the train, when I realised that it was a slow train and that the express had gone three hours before while we had been pacing the hall of the guest house with our luggage packed and nobody coming for us, the spirit came upon me and my lips were unsealed. I spoke to my guide, as one mariner might speak to another, and told him what I thought of Russian methods. He listened with the profoundest respect to my rich incisive phrases. When at last I paused, he replied—in words that are also significant of certain weaknesses of the present Russian state of mind. " You see," he said, " the blockade ——"

But if I saw nothing of Lunacharsky personally, I saw something of the work

H

he has organised. The primary material
of the educationist is human beings, and
of these at least there is still no shortage
in Russia, so that in that respect Lunacharsky is better off than most of his
colleagues. And beginning with an initial
prejudice and much distrust, I am bound
to confess that, in view of their enormous
difficulties, the educational work of the
Bolsheviks impresses me as being as-
tonishingly good.

Things started badly. Directly I got to
Petersburg I asked to see a school, and
on the second day of my visit I was taken
to one that impressed me very unfavourably.
It was extremely well equipped, much
better than an ordinary English grammar
school, and the children were bright and
intelligent ; but our visit fell in the recess.
I could witness no teaching, and the
behaviour of the youngsters I saw indicated a low standard of discipline. I
formed an opinion that I was probably
being shown a picked school specially
prepared for me, and that this was all that

Petersburg had to offer. The special guide who was with us then began to question these children upon the subject of English literature and the writers they liked most. One name dominated all others. My own. Such comparatively trivial figures as Milton, Dickens, Shakespeare ran about intermittently between the feet of that literary colossus. Being questioned further, these children produced the titles of perhaps a dozen of my books. I said I was completely satisfied by what I had seen and heard, that I wanted to see nothing more—for indeed what more could I possibly require ?—and I left that school smiling with difficulty and thoroughly cross with my guides.

Three days later I suddenly scrapped my morning's engagements and insisted upon being taken at once to another school—any school close at hand. I was convinced that I had been deceived about the former school, and that now I should see a very bad school indeed. Instead I saw a much better one than the first I had seen. The equipment and building were better, the discipline of the children was better, and I saw some excellent teaching in progress. Most of the teachers were women, very competent-looking middle-aged women, and I chose elementary geometrical teaching to observe because that on the blackboard is in the universal language of the diagram. I saw also a heap of drawings and various models the pupils had done, and they were very good. The school was supplied with abundant pictures. I noted particularly a well-chosen series of landscapes to assist the geographical teaching. There was plenty of chemical and physical apparatus, and it was evidently put to a proper use. I also saw the children's next meal in preparation—for children eat at school in Soviet Russia –and the food was excellent and well cooked, far above the standard of the adult rations we had seen served out. All this was much more satisfactory. Finally by a few questions we tested the extraordinary vogue of H. G. Wells among

the young people of Russia. None of
these children had ever heard of him.
The school library contained none of his
books. This did much to convince me
that I was seeing a quite normal school.
I had, I now begin to realise, been taken
to the previous one not, as I had supposed
in my wrath, with any elaborate intention
of deceiving me about the state of education in the country, but after certain
kindly intrigues and preparations by a
literary friend, Mr. Chukovsky the critic,
affectionately anxious to make me feel
myself beloved in Russia, and a little
oblivious of the real gravity of the business
I had in hand.

Subsequent enquiries and comparison of
my observations with those of other visitors
to Russia, and particularly those of Dr.
Haden Guest, who also made surprise
visits to several schools in Moscow, have
convinced me that Soviet Russia, in the
face of gigantic difficulties, has made and
is making very great educational efforts,
and that in spite of the difficulties of the

general situation the quality and number
of the schools *in the towns* has risen absolutely since the Tsarist *régime.* (The
peasant, as ever, except in a few " show "
localities, remains scarcely touched by
these things.) The schools I saw would
have been good middle schools in England.
They are open to all, and there is an
attempt to make education compulsory.
Of course Russia has its peculiar difficulties.
Many of the schools are understaffed,
and it is difficult to secure the attendance
of unwilling pupils. Numbers of children
prefer to keep out of the schools and
trade upon the streets. A large part of
the illicit trading in Russia is done by
bands of children. They are harder to
catch than adults, and the spirit of Russian
Communism is against punishing them.
And the Russian child is, for a northern
child, remarkably precocious.

The common practice of co-educating
youngsters up to fifteen or sixteen, in a
country as demoralised as Russia is now,
has brought peculiar evils in its train.

My attention was called to this by the visit of Bokaiev, the former head of the Petersburg Extraordinary Commission, and his colleague Zalutsky to Gorky to consult him in the matter. They discussed their business in front of me quite frankly, and the whole conversation was translated to me as it went on. The Bolshevik authorities have collected and published very startling, very shocking figures of the moral condition of young people in Petersburg, which I have seen. How far they would compare with the British figures—if there are any British figures—of such bad districts for the young as are some parts of East London or such towns of low type employment as Reading I do not know. (The reader should compare the Fabian Society's report on prostitution, *Downward Paths*, upon this question.) Nor do I know how they would show in comparison with preceding Tsarist conditions. Nor can I speculate how far these phenomena in Russia are the mechanical consequence of privation and overcrowding in a home atmosphere bordering on despair. But there can be no doubt that in the Russian towns, concurrently with increased educational effort and an enhanced intellectual stimulation of the young, there is also an increased lawlessness on their part, especially in sexual matters, and that this is going on in a phase of unexampled sobriety and harsh puritanical decorum so far as adult life is concerned. This hectic moral fever of the young is the dark side of the educational spectacle in Russia. I think it is to be regarded mainly as an aspect of the general social collapse ; every European country has noted a parallel moral relaxation of the young under the war strain ; but the revolution itself, in sweeping a number of the old experienced teachers out of the schools and in making every moral standard a subject of debate, has no doubt contributed also to an as yet incalculable amount in the excessive disorder of these matters in present-day Russia.

Faced with this problem of starving and

GUESTS AT THE HOME OF REST FOR WORKMEN ON THE KAMENNI OSTROF.

shattered homes and a social chaos, the Bolshevik organisers are *institutionalising* the town children of Russia. They are making their schools residential. The children of the Russian urban population are going, like the children of the British upper class, into boarding schools. Close to this second school I visited stood two big buildings which are the living places of the boys and of the girls respectively. In these places they can be kept under some sort of hygienic and moral discipline. This again happens to be not only in accordance with Communist doctrine, but with the special necessities of the Russian crisis. Entire towns are sinking down towards slum conditions, and the Bolshevik Government has had to play the part of a gigantic Dr. Barnardo.

We went over the organisation of a sort of reception home to which children are brought by their parents who find it impossible to keep them clean and decent and nourished under the terrible conditions outside. This reception home is the old

Hotel de l'Europe, the scene of countless
pleasant little dinner-parties under the old
régime.   On the roof there is still the
summertime roof garden, where the string
quartette used to play, and on the staircase
we passed a frosted glass window still
bearing in gold letters the words *Coiffure
des Dames*.

Slender gilded pointing hands directed
us to the " Restaurant," long vanished from
the grim Petersburg scheme of things.
Into this place the children come ; they
pass into a special quarantine section for
infectious diseases and for personal cleanli-
ness—nine-tenths of the newcomers har-
bour unpleasant parasites—and then into
another section, the moral quarantine,
where for a time they are watched for bad
habits and undesirable tendencies.   From
this section some individuals may need to
be weeded out and sent to special schools
for defectives.   The rest pass on into
the general body of institutionalised
children, and so on to the boarding
schools.

Here certainly we have the " break-up
of the family " in full progress, and the
Bolshevik net is sweeping wide and taking
in children of the most miscellaneous
origins. The parents have reasonably free
access to their children in the daytime, but
little or no control over their education,
clothing, or the like. We went among the
children in the various stages of this
educational process, and they seemed to
us to be quite healthy, happy, and contented children. But they get very good
people to look after them. Many men and
women, politically suspects or openly dis-
contented with the existing political conditions, and yet with a desire to serve
Russia, have found in these places work
that they can do with a good heart and
conscience. My interpreter and the lady
who took us round this place had often
dined and supped in the Hotel de l'Europe
in its brilliant days, and they knew each
other well. This lady was now plainly clad,
with short cut hair and a grave manner ;
her husband was a White and serving with

the Poles ; she had two children of her own
in the institution, and she was mothering
some scores of little creatures. But she
was evidently keenly proud of the work of
her organisation, and she said that she
found life—in this city of want, under the
shadow of a coming famine—more interesting and satisfying than it had ever been in
the old days.

I have no space to tell of other educational work we saw going on in Russia.
I can give but a word or so to the Home of
Rest for Workmen in the Kamenni Ostrof.
I thought that at once rather fine and not a
little absurd. To this place workers are
sent to live a life of refined ease for two or
three weeks. It is a very beautiful country
house with big gardens, an orangery, and
subordinate buildings. The meals are
served on white cloths with flowers upon
the table and so forth. And the worker
has to live up to these elegant surroundings.
It is a part of his education. If in a forget-
ful moment he clears his throat in the
good old resonant peasant manner and

spits upon the floor, an attendant, I was told, chalks a circle about his defilement and obliges him to clean the offended parquetry. The avenue approaching this place has been adorned with decoration in the futurist style, and there is a vast figure of a " worker " at the gates resting on his hammer, done in gypsum, which was obtained from the surgical reserves of the Petersburg hospitals. . . . But after all, the idea of civilising your workpeople by dipping them into pleasant surroundings is, in itself, rather a good one. . . .

I find it difficult to hold the scales of justice upon many of these efforts of Bolshevism. Here are these creative and educational things going on, varying between the admirable and the ridiculous, islands at least of cleanly work and, I think, of hope, amidst the vast spectacle of grisly want and wide decay. Who can weigh the power and possibility of their thrust against the huge gravitation of this sinking system ? Who can guess what encouragement and enhancement they may get if Russia can win through to a respite from civil and foreign warfare and from famine and want? It was of this re-created Russia, this Russia that may be, that I was most desirous of talking when I went to the Kremlin to meet Lenin. Of that conversation I will tell in my final chapter.

V. The Petersburg Soviet

ON Thursday the 7th of October we attended a meeting of the Petersburg Soviet. We were told that we should find this a very different legislative body from the British House of Commons, and we did. Like nearly everything else in the arrangements of Soviet Russia it struck us as extraordinarily unpremeditated and improvised. Nothing could have been less intelligently planned for the functions it had to perform or the responsibilities it had to undertake.

The meeting was held in the old Winter Garden of the Tauride Palace, the former palace of Potemkin, the favourite of Catherine the Second. Here the Imperial Duma met under the Tsarist *régime*, and I visited it in 1914 and saw a languid session in progress. I went then with Mr. Maurice Baring and one of the Benckendorffs to the strangers' gallery, which ran round three sides of the hall. There was accommodation for perhaps a thousand people in the hall, and most of it was empty. The president with his bell sat above a rostrum, and behind him was a row of women reporters. I do not now remember what business was in hand on that occasion ; it was certainly not very exciting business. Baring, I remember, pointed out the large proportion of priests elected to the third Duma ; their beards and cassocks made a distinctive feature of that scattered gathering.

On this second visit we were no longer stranger onlookers, but active participants in the meeting ; we came into the body of the hall behind the president's bench, where on a sort of stage the members of the Government, official visitors, and so forth find accommodation. The presidential bench, the rostrum, and the reporters remained, but instead of an atmosphere of weary parliamentarianism, we found ourselves in the crowding, the noise, and the

peculiar thrill of a mass meeting. There
were, I should think, some two hundred
people or more packed upon the semi-
circular benches round about us on the
platform behind the president, comrades
in naval uniforms and in middle-class and
working-class costume, numerous intelli-
gent-looking women, one or two Asiatics
and a few unclassifiable visitors, and the
body of the hall beyond the presidential
bench was densely packed with people who
filled not only the seats but the gangways
and the spaces under the galleries. There
may have been two or three thousand people
down there, men and women. They were
all members of the Petersburg Soviet,
which is really a sort of conjoint meeting
of its constituent soviets. The visitors'
galleries above were equally full.

Above the rostrum, with his back to us,
sat Zenovieff, his right-hand man Zorin,
and the president. The subject under
discussion was the proposed peace with
Poland. The meeting was smarting with
the sense of defeat and disposed to resent

I 2

the Polish terms. Soon after we came in
Zenovieff made a long and, so far as I could
judge, a very able speech, preparing the
minds of this great gathering for a Russian
surrender.   The Polish demands were out-
rageous, but for the present Russia must
submit.   He was followed by an oldish
man who made a bitter attack upon the
irreligion of the people and government of
Russia ; Russia was suffering for her sins,
and until she repented and returned to
religion she would continue to suffer one
disaster after another.   His opinions were
not those of the meeting, but he was
allowed to have his say without interruption.
The decision to make peace with Poland
was then taken by a show of hands.   Then
came my little turn.   The meeting was told
that I had come from England to see the
Bolshevik *régime ;* I was praised profusely ;
I was also exhorted to treat that *régime*
fairly and not to emulate those other recent
visitors (these were Mrs. Snowden and
Guest and Bertrand Russell) who had
enjoyed the hospitality of the republic and

then gone away to say unfavourable things of it. This exhortation left me cold ; I had come to Russia to judge the Bolshevik Government and not to praise it. I had then to take possession of the rostrum and address this big crowd of people. This rostrum I knew had proved an unfortunate place for one or two previous visitors, who had found it hard to explain away afterwards the speeches their translators had given the world through the medium of the wireless reports. Happily, I had had some inkling of what was coming. To avoid any misunderstanding I had written out a short speech in English, and I had had this translated carefully into Russian. I began by saying clearly that I was neither Marxist nor Communist, but a Collectivist, and that it was not to a social revolution in the West that Russians should look for peace and help in their troubles, but to the liberal opinion of the moderate mass of Western people. I declared that the people of the Western States were determined to give Russia

peace, so that she might develop upon her
own lines. Their own line of development
might be very different from that of
Russia. When I had done I handed a
translation of my speech to my interpreter,
Zorin, which not only eased his task but
did away with any possibility of a subsequent misunderstanding. My speech was
reported in the *Pravda* quite fully and
fairly.

Then followed a motion by Zorin that
Zenovieff should have leave to visit Berlin
and attend the conference of the Independent Socialists there. Zorin is a witty and
humorous speaker, and he got his audience
into an excellent frame of mind. His
motion was carried by a show of hands,
and then came a report and a discussion
upon the production of vegetables in the
Petersburg district. It was a practical
question upon which feeling ran high.
Here speakers rose in the body of the hall,
discharging brief utterances for a minute
or so and subsiding again. There were
shouts and interruptions. The debate was

much more like a big labour mass meeting
in the Queen's Hall than anything that a
Western European would recognise as a
legislature.

This business disposed of, a still more
extraordinary thing happened. We who
sat behind the rostrum poured down into
the already very crowded body of the hall
and got such seats as we could find, and
a white sheet was lowered behind the
president's seat. At the same time a band
appeared in the gallery to the left. A
five-part cinematograph film was then run,
showing the Baku Conference to which I
have already alluded. The pictures were
viewed with interest but without any
violent applause. And at the end the band
played the *Internationale*, and the audience
—I beg its pardon !—the Petersburg Soviet
dispersed singing that popular chant. It
was in fact a mass meeting incapable of
any real legislative activities ; capable at
the utmost of endorsing or not endorsing
the Government in control of the platform. Compared with the British Parlia-

ment it has about as much organisation, structure, and working efficiency as a big bagful of miscellaneous wheels might have, compared to an old-fashioned and inaccurate but still going clock.

THE PETERSBURG SOVIET IN SESSION.

Lenin at the rostrum; below him are the women stenographers; immediately behind him is Zenovieff and the President. Behind these again are officials and ministerial persons, official visitors and the like.

VI. The Dreamer in the Kremlin

MY chief purpose in going from Petersburg to Moscow was to see and talk to Lenin. I was very curious to see him, and I was disposed to be hostile to him. I encountered a personality entirely different from anything I had expected to meet.

Lenin is not a writer ; his published work does not express him. The shrill little pamphlets and papers issued from Moscow in his name, full of misconceptions of the labour psychology of the West and obstinately defensive of the impossible proposition that it is the prophesied Marxist social revolution which has happened in Russia, display hardly anything of the real Lenin mentality as I encountered it. Occasionally there are gleams of an inspired shrewdness, but for the rest these publications do no more than rehearse the set ideas and phrases of doctrinaire Marxism. Perhaps that is necessary. That may be the only language Communism understands ; a break into a new dialect would be disturbing and demoralising. Left Communism is the backbone of Russia to-day ; unhappily it is a backbone without flexible joints, a backbone that can be bent only with the utmost difficulty and which must be bent by means of flattery and deference.

Moscow under the bright October sunshine, amidst the fluttering yellow leaves, impressed us as being altogether more lax and animated than Petersburg. There is much more movement of people, more trading, and a comparative plenty of droshkys. Markets are open. There is not the same general ruination of streets and houses. There are, it is true, many traces of the desperate street fighting of early 1918. One of the domes of that absurd cathedral of St. Basil just outside the Kremlin gate was smashed by a shell and still awaits repair. The tramcars we found were not carrying passengers ; they were being used for the transport of supplies of food and fuel. In these matters Petersburg claims to be better prepared than Moscow.

The ten thousand crosses of Moscow still glitter in the afternoon light. On one conspicuous pinnacle of the Kremlin the imperial eagles spread their wings ; the Bolshevik Government has been too busy or too indifferent to pull them down. The churches are open, the kissing of ikons is a flourishing industry, and beggars still woo casual charity at the doors. The celebrated miraculous shrine of the Iberian Madonna outside the Redeemer Gate was particularly busy. There were many peasant women, unable to get into the little chapel, kissing the stones outside.

Just opposite to it, on a plaster panel on a house front, is that now celebrated inscription put up by one of the early revolutionary administrations in Moscow : " Religion is the Opium of the People." The effect this inscription produces is greatly reduced by the fact that in Russia the people cannot read.

About that inscription I had a slight but amusing argument with Mr. Vanderlip, the American financier, who was lodged in the same guest house as ourselves. He wanted to have it effaced. I was for retaining it as being historically interesting, and because I think that religious toleration should extend to atheists. But Mr. Vanderlip felt too strongly to see the point of that.

The Moscow Guest House, which we shared with Mr. Vanderlip and an adventurous English artist who had somehow got through to Moscow to execute busts of Lenin and Trotsky, was a big, richly-furnished house upon the Sofiskaya Naberezhnaya (No. 17), directly facing the great wall of the Kremlin and all the clustering domes and pinnacles of that imperial inner city. We felt much less free and more secluded here than in Petersburg. There were sentinels at the gates to protect us from casual visitors,

whereas in Petersburg all sorts of un-
authorised persons could and did stray in
to talk to me. Mr. Vanderlip had been
staying here, I gathered, for some weeks,
and proposed to stay some weeks more.
He was without valet, secretary, or interpreter. He did not discuss his business
with me beyond telling me rather carefully once or twice that it was strictly
financial and commercial and in no sense
political. I was told that he had brought
credentials from Senator Harding to Lenin,
but I am temperamentally incurious and
I made no attempt whatever to verify this
statement or to pry into Mr. Vanderlip's
affairs. I did not even ask how it could
be possible to conduct business or financial
operations in a Communist State with
any one but the Government, nor how it
was possible to deal with a Government
upon strictly non-political lines. These
were, I admitted, mysteries beyond my
understanding. But we ate, smoked, drank
our coffee and conversed together in an
atmosphere of profound discretion. By

not mentioning Mr. Vanderlip's "mission," we made it a portentous, omnipresent fact.

The arrangements leading up to my meeting with Lenin were tedious and irritating, but at last I found myself under way for the Kremlin in the company of Mr. Rothstein, formerly a figure in London Communist circles, and an American comrade with a large camera who was also, I gathered, an official of the Russian Foreign Office.

The Kremlin as I remembered it in 1914 was a very open place, open much as Windsor Castle is, with a thin trickle of pilgrims and tourists in groups and couples flowing through it. But now it is closed up and difficult of access. There was a great pother with passes and permits before we could get through even the outer gates. And we were filtered and inspected through five or six rooms of clerks and sentinels before we got into the presence. This may be necessary for the personal security of Lenin, but it puts him out of reach of Russia, and, what perhaps is more serious, if there is to be an effectual dictatorship, it puts Russia out of his reach. If things must filter up to him, they must also filter down, and they may undergo very considerable changes in the process.

We got to Lenin at last and found him, a little figure at a great desk in a well-lit room that looked out upon palatial spaces. I thought his desk was rather in a litter. I sat down on a chair at a corner of the desk, and the little man—his feet scarcely touch the ground as he sits on the edge of his chair—twisted round to talk to me, putting his arms round and over a pile of papers. He spoke excellent English, but it was, I thought, rather characteristic of the present condition of Russian affairs that Mr. Rothstein chaperoned the conversation, occasionally offering footnotes and other assistance. Meanwhile the American got to work with his camera, and unobtrusively but persistently exposed plates. The talk, however, was too interesting for

K

that to be an annoyance. One forgot about that clicking and shifting about quite soon.

I had come expecting to struggle with a doctrinaire Marxist. I found nothing of the sort. I had been told that Lenin lectured people ; he certainly did not do so on this occasion. Much has been made of his laugh in the descriptions, a laugh which is said to be pleasing at first and afterwards to become cynical. This laugh was not in evidence. His forehead reminded me of someone else—I could not remember who it was, until the other evening I saw Mr. Arthur Balfour sitting and talking under a shaded light. It is exactly the same domed, slightly one-sided cranium. Lenin has a pleasant, quick-changing, brownish face, with a lively smile and a habit (due perhaps to some defect in focussing) of screwing up one eye as he pauses in his talk ; he is not very like the photographs you see of him because he is one of those people whose change of expression is more important than their features ; he gesticulated a little with his hands over the heaped papers as he talked, and he talked quickly, very keen on his subject, without any posing or pretences or reservations, as a good type of scientific man will talk.

Our talk was threaded throughout and held together by two—what shall I call them ?—*motifs*. One was from me to him : " What do you think you are making of Russia ? What is the state you are trying to create ? " The other was from him to me : " Why does not the social revolution begin in England ? Why do you not work for the social revolution ? Why are you not destroying Capitalism and establishing the Communist State ? " These *motifs* interwove, reacted on each other, illuminated each other. The second brought back the first : " But what are you making of the social revolution ? Are you making a success of it ? " And from that we got back to two again with : " To make it a success the Western world must join in. Why doesn't it ? "

In the days before 1918 all the Marxist
world thought of the social revolution as
an end. The workers of the world were to
unite, overthrow Capitalism, and be happy
ever afterwards. But in 1918 the Communists, to their own surprise, found themselves in control of Russia and challenged
to produce their millennium. They have a
colourable excuse for a delay in the production of a new and better social order
in their continuation of war conditions, in
the blockade and so forth, nevertheless it
is clear that they begin to realise the
tremendous unpreparedness which the
Marxist methods of thought involve. At
a hundred points—I have already put a
finger upon one or two of them—they
do not know what to do. But the common-
place Communist simply loses his temper
if you venture to doubt whether everything is being done in precisely the best
and most intelligent way under the new
régime. He is like a tetchy housewife
who wants you to recognise that everything is in perfect order in the middle of

an eviction. He is like one of those now forgotten suffragettes who used to promise us an earthly paradise as soon as we escaped from the tyranny of " man-made laws." Lenin, on the other hand, whose frankness must at times leave his disciples breathless, has recently stripped off the last pretence that the Russian revolution is anything more than the inauguration of an age of limitless experiment. " Those who are engaged in the formidable task of overcoming capitalism," he has recently written, " must be prepared to try method after method until they find the one which answers their purpose best."

We opened our talk with a discussion of the future of the great towns under Communism. I wanted to see how far Lenin contemplated the dying out of the towns in Russia. The desolation of Petersburg had brought home to me a point I had never realised before, that the whole form and arrangement of a town is determined by shopping and marketing, and that the abolition of these things renders nine-tenths of the buildings in an ordinary town directly or indirectly unmeaning and useless. " The towns will get very much smaller," he admitted. " They will be different. Yes, quite different." That, I suggested, implied a tremendous task. It meant the scrapping of the existing towns and their replacement. The churches and great buildings of Petersburg would become presently like those of Novgorod the Great or like the temples of Paestum. Most of the town would dissolve away. He agreed quite cheerfully. I think it warmed his heart to find someone who understood a necessary consequence of collectivism that many even of his own people fail to grasp. Russia has to be rebuilt fundamentally, has to become a new thing. . . .

And industry has to be reconstructed— as fundamentally ?

Did I realise what was already in hand with Russia ? The electrification of Russia ?

For Lenin, who like a good orthodox

Marxist denounces all " Utopians," has succumbed at last to a Utopia, the Utopia of the electricians. He is throwing all his weight into a scheme for the development of great power stations in Russia to serve whole provinces with light, with transport, and industrial power. Two experimental districts he said had already been electrified. Can one imagine a more courageous project in a vast flat land of forests and illiterate peasants, with no water power, with no technical skill available, and with trade and industry at the last gasp ? Projects for such an electrification are in process of development in Holland and they have been discussed in England, and in those densely-populated and industrially highly-developed centres one can imagine them as successful, economical, and altogether beneficial. But their application to Russia is an altogether greater strain upon the constructive imagination. I cannot see anything of the sort happening in this dark crystal of Russia, but this little man at the Kremlin can ; he sees the decaying railways replaced by a new electric transport, sees new roadways spreading throughout the land, sees a new and happier Communist industrialism arising again. While I talked to him he almost persuaded me to share his vision.

" And you will go on to these things with the peasants rooted in your soil ? "

But not only are the towns to be rebuilt ; every agricultural landmark is to go.

" Even now," said Lenin, " all the agricultural production of Russia is not peasant production. We have, in places, large scale agriculture. The Government is already running big estates with workers instead of peasants, where conditions are favourable. That can spread. It can be extended first to one province, then another. The peasants in the other provinces, selfish and illiterate, will not know what is happening until their turn comes. . . ."

It may be difficult to defeat the Russian peasant *en masse ;* but in detail there is no difficulty at all. At the mention of the peasant Lenin's head came nearer to

LENIN.

Behind him stands Gorky ; to the right of Gorky (*i.e.* on his left)
are Zorin (*hat*) and Zenovieff. Behind with cigarette is Radek.

mine ; his manner became confidential. As if after all the peasant *might* over-hear.

It is not only the material organisation of society you have to build, I argued, it is the mentality of a whole people. The Russian people are by habit and tradition traders and individualists ; their very souls must be remoulded if this new world is to be achieved. Lenin asked me what I had seen of the educational work afoot. I praised some of the things I had seen. He nodded and smiled with pleasure. He has an unlimited confidence in his work.

" But these are only sketches and beginnings," I said.

" Come back and see what we have done in Russia in ten years' time," he answered.

In him I realised that Communism could after all, in spite of Marx, be enormously creative. After the tiresome class-war fanatics I had been encountering among the Communists, men of formulæ as sterile as flints, after numerous experiences of the trained and empty conceit of the common Marxist devotee, this amazing little man, with his frank admission of the immensity and complication of the project of Communism and his simple concentration upon its realisation, was very refreshing. He at least has a vision of a world changed over and planned and built afresh.

He wanted more of my Russian impressions. I told him that I thought that in many directions, and more particularly in the Petersburg Commune, Communism was pressing too hard and too fast, and destroying before it was ready to rebuild. They had broken down trading before they were ready to ration ; the co-operative organisation had been smashed up instead of being utilised, and so on. That brought us to our essential difference, the difference of the Evolutionary Collectivist and Marxist, the question whether the social revolution is, in its extremity, necessary, whether it is necessary to overthrow one economic system completely before the new one can begin. I believe that through a vast sustained educational campaign the existing Capitalist system can be *civilised* into a Collectivist world system ; Lenin on the other hand tied himself years ago to the Marxist dogmas of the inevitable class war, the downfall of Capitalist order as a prelude to reconstruction, the proletarian dictatorship, and so forth. He had to argue, therefore, that modern Capitalism is incurably predatory, wasteful, and un-teachable, and that until it is destroyed it will continue to exploit the human heritage stupidly and aimlessly, that it will fight against and prevent any administra-tion of natural resources for the general good, and that, because essentially it is a scramble, it will inevitably make wars.

I had, I will confess, a very uphill argument. He suddenly produced Chiozza Money's new book, *The Triumph of Nationalisation*, which he had evidently been reading very carefully. " But you see directly you begin to have a good working collectivist organisation of any public interest, the Capitalists smash it up

again. They smashed your national ship-
yards ; they won't let you work your coal
economically." He tapped the book. " It
is all here."

And against my argument that wars
sprang from nationalist imperialism and not
from a Capitalist organisation of society
he suddenly brought : " But what do you
think of this new Republican Imperialism
that comes to us from America ? "

Here Mr. Rothstein intervened in
Russian with an objection that Lenin
swept aside.

And regardless of Mr. Rothstein's plea
for diplomatic reserve, Lenin proceeded
to explain the projects with which one
American at least was seeking to dazzle
the imagination of Moscow. There was
to be economic assistance for Russia and
recognition of the Bolshevik Government.
There was to be a defensive alliance against
Japanese aggression in Siberia. There was
to be an American naval station on the
coast of Asia, and leases for long terms of
sixty or fifty years of the natural resources

of Khamskhatka and possibly of other large regions of Russian Asia. Well, did I think that made for peace ? Was it anything more than the beginning of a new world scramble ? How would the British Imperialists like this sort of thing ?

Always, he insisted, Capitalism competes and scrambles. It is the antithesis of collective action. It cannot develop into social unity or into world unity.

But some industrial power had to come in and help Russia, I said. She cannot reconstruct now without such help. . . .

Our multifarious argumentation ended indecisively. We parted warmly, and I and my companion were filtered out of the Kremlin through one barrier after another in much the same fashion as we had been filtered in.

" He is wonderful," said Mr. Rothstein. " But it was an indiscretion ——"

I was not disposed to talk as we made our way, under the glowing trees that grow in the ancient moat of the Kremlin, back to our Guest House. I wanted to

think Lenin over while I had him fresh
in my mind, and I did not want to
be assisted by the expositions of my companion. But Mr. Rothstein kept on talking.

He was still pressing me not to mention
this little sketch of the Russian-American
outlook to Mr. Vanderlip long after I
assured him that I respected Mr. Vanderlip's veil of discretion far too much to
pierce it by any careless word.

And so back to No. 17 Sofiskaya
Naberezhnaya, and lunch with Mr. Vanderlip and the young sculptor from London.
The old servant of the house waited on
us, mournfully conscious of the meagreness
of our entertainment and reminiscent of
the great days of the past when Caruso
had been a guest and had sung to all that
was brilliant in Moscow in the room up-
stairs. Mr. Vanderlip was for visiting the
big market that afternoon — and later
going to the Ballet, but my son and I were
set upon returning to Petersburg that
night and so getting on to Reval in time
for the Stockholm boat.

VII. The Envoy

VII. The Envoy

IN the preceding chapters I have written in the first person and in a familiar style because I did not want the reader to lose sight for a moment of the shortness of our visit to Russia and of my personal limitations. Now in conclusion, if the reader will have patience with me for a few final words, I would like in less personal terms and very plainly to set down my main convictions about the Russian situation. They are deep-seated convictions, and they concern not merely Russia but the whole present outlook of our civilisation. They are merely one man's opinion, but as I feel them strongly, so I put them without weakening qualifications.

First, then, Russia, which was a modern civilisation of the Western type, least disciplined and most ramshackle of all the Great Powers, is now a modern civilisation *in extremis*. The direct cause of its downfall has been modern war leading to physical exhaustion. Only through that could the Bolsheviks have secured power. Nothing like this Russian downfall has ever happened before. If it goes on for a year or so more the process of collapse will be complete. Nothing will be left of Russia but a country of peasants ; the towns will be practically deserted and in ruins, the railways will be rusting in disuse. With the railways will go the last vestiges of any general government. The peasants are absolutely illiterate and collectively stupid, capable of resisting interference but incapable of comprehensive foresight and organisation. They will become a sort of human swamp in a state of division, petty civil war, and political squalour, with a famine whenever the harvests are bad ; and they will be breeding epidemics for the rest of Europe. They will lapse towards Asia.

The collapse of the civilised system in

Russia into peasant barbarism means that
Europe will be cut off for many years from
all the mineral wealth of Russia, and from
any supply of raw products from this
area, from its corn, flax, and the like. It
is an open question whether the Western
Powers can get along without these supplies. Their cessation certainly means
a general impoverishment of Western
Europe.

The only possible Government that can
stave off such a final collapse of Russia now
is the present Bolshevik Government, if it
can be assisted by America and the
Western Powers. There is now no alternative to that Government possible. There
are of course a multitude of antagonists—
adventurers and the like—ready, with
European assistance, to attempt the overthrow of that Bolshevik Government, but
there are no signs of any common purpose
and moral unity capable of replacing it.
And moreover there is no time now for
another revolution in Russia. A year
more of civil war will make the final

sinking of Russia out of civilisation inevitable. We have to make what we can,
therefore, of the Bolshevik Government,
whether we like it or not.

The Bolshevik Government is inexperienced and incapable to an extreme degree ;
it has had phases of violence and cruelty ;
but it is on the whole honest. And it
includes a few individuals of real creative
imagination and power, who may with
opportunity, if their hands are strengthened,
achieve great reconstructions. The Bolshevik Government seems on the whole to
be trying to act up to its professions, which
are still held by most of its supporters with
a quite religious passion. Given generous
help, it may succeed in establishing a new
social order in Russia of a civilised type
with which the rest of the world will be
able to deal. It will probably be a miti-
gated Communism, with a large-scale
handling of transport, industry, and (later)
agriculture.

It is necessary that we should understand and respect the professions and

principles of the Bolsheviks if we Western peoples are to be of any effectual service to humanity in Russia. Hitherto these professions and principles have been ignored in the most extraordinary way by the Western Governments. The Bolshevik Government is, and says it is, a Communist Government. And it means this, and will make this the standard of its conduct. It has suppressed private ownership and private trade in Russia, not as an act of expediency but as an act of right ; and in all Russia there remain now no commercial individuals and bodies with whom we can deal who will respect the conventions and usages of Western commercial life. The Bolshevik Government, we have to understand, has, by its nature, an invincible prejudice against individual business men ; it will not treat them in a manner that they will consider fair and honourable ; it will distrust them and, as far as it can, put them at the completest disadvantage. It regards them as pirates— or at best as privateers. It is hopeless and impossible therefore for individual persons and firms to think of going into Russia to trade. There is only one being in Russia with whom the Western world can deal, and that is the Bolshevik Government itself, and there is no way of dealing with that one being safely and effectually except through some national or, better, some international Trust. This latter body, which might represent some single Power or group of Powers, or which might even have some titular connection with the League of Nations, would be able to deal with the Bolshevik Government on equal terms. It would have to recognise the Bolshevik Government and, in conjunction with it, to set about the now urgent task of the material restoration of civilised life in European and Asiatic Russia. It should resemble in its general nature one of the big buying and controlling trusts that were so necessary and effectual in the European States during the Great War. It should deal with its individual producers on the one hand, and

the Bolshevik Government would deal
with its own population on the other.
Such a Trust could speedily make itself
indispensable to the Bolshevik Government. This indeed is the only way in
which a capitalist State can hold commerce
with a Communist State. The attempts
that have been made during the past year
and more to devise some method of private
trading in Russia without recognition
of the Bolshevik Government were
from the outset as hopeless as the
search for the North-West passage from
England to India. The channels are
frozen up.

Any country or group of countries with
adequate industrial resources which goes
into Bolshevik Russia with recognition and
help will necessarily become the supporter,
the right hand, and the consultant of the
Bolshevik Government. It will react upon
that Government and be reacted upon. It
will probably become more collectivist in
its methods, and, on the other hand, the
rigours of extreme Communism in Russia

will probably be greatly tempered through its influence.

The only Power capable of playing this *rôle* of eleventh-hour helper to Russia single-handed is the United States of America. That is why I find the adventure of the enterprising and imaginative Mr. Vanderlip very significant. I doubt the conclusiveness of his negotiations; they are probably only the opening phase of a discussion of the Russian problem upon a new basis that may lead it at last to a comprehensive world treatment of this situation. Other Powers than the United States will, in the present phase of world-exhaustion, need to combine before they can be of any effective use to Russia. Big business is by no means antipathetic to Communism. The larger big business grows the more it approximates to Collectivism. It is the upper road of the few instead of the lower road of the masses to Collectivism.

The only alternative to such a helpful intervention in Bolshevik Russia is, I firmly believe, the final collapse of all that remains of modern civilisation throughout what was formerly the Russian Empire. It is highly improbable that the collapse will be limited to its boundaries. Both eastward and westward other great regions may, one after another, tumble into the big hole in civilisation thus created. Possibly all modern civilisation may tumble in.

These propositions do not refer to any hypothetical future ; they are an attempt to state the outline facts and possibilities of what is going on—and going on with great rapidity—in Russia and in the world generally now, as they present themselves to my mind. This in general terms is the frame of circumstance in which I would have the sketches of Russia that have preceded this set and read. So it is I interpret the writing on the Eastern wall of Europe.

PRINTED IN GREAT BRITAIN BY
RICHARD CLAY AND SONS, LIMITED,
BRUNSWICK STREET, STAMFORD STREET, S.E. 1,
AND BUNGAY, SUFFOLK.